Nothing To Do With Me

Nothing To Do With Me

Poems

By Sarah Xerta

This book published by University of Hell Press.
www.universityofhellpress.com

Cover Design and Layout by Vince Norris
www.norrisportfolio.com

Cover Art and Illustrations by Susannah Kelly
www.susannahkellyart.com

Published in the United States of America.
ISBN 978-1-938753-14-5

Contents

Hello Hello 9
RSVP 11
This Morning the Dew on the Grass Was so Beautiful 12
Daisies the Size of Moons 14
Crush 17
Coil 19
November 22
All the Birthday Candles 24
If This Were a Protest My Sign Would Be Blank 26
While I'm Busy 28
Birth Poem 30
Smoke 32
Down into the Grass 34
Pretty Head 37
Unborn 39
Professionals 42
Revolution 44
Everything Beautiful Happens in My Mouth 48
Red Paper Heart 51
Big Spoon I Keep Wetting My Lips Against 53
American Spirit 56
Moon Dog 58

To a Real Party 63
This Is What It's like to Fall out of Love 65

Rain Poem 66
The Soft Dark 69
The Smaller I Become in It 72
American Mouth 74
All the Birds from the Trees 76
Whoever Decided It Was a Good Idea for Lovers to Cohabitate 78
Someone Left out in the Rain 80
The Wake 82
The Morning after I Left 84
Blood Lines 86
On Elbows 88
Pinot Noir 90
When People Ask If I'm Going to Give Evelyn a Brother or Sister 92
Bear 93
Bruises 96
Sad Circus Tents 99
Cat Lady 101
The Shape of a Heart 103
May 105
Party of One 107

Acknowledgements 110

meanwhile in my head
I'm undergoing open-heart surgery.

—Anne Sexton

Hello Hello

Poets are some of the emptiest people I know
is a thought that just hit me from somewhere in the back
of my brain, those shithead elves throwing snowballs at me.
My armpits are damp because I've spent
the morning alone on my couch, thinking about strands
of words like pearls, how much I want to kiss
every collarbone in the world. How much I miss you.
I can't remember the last time I saw a bird or
fingered myself, and now the morning is over and I'm still
on the couch, my belly full of pasta, my Christmas lights on and
my heart so steady I can feel it in my clit, that humming-
bird tongue where the tops of my thighs meet.
What are you doing and why isn't it me?
I'm trying to let go of the person I am.
I'm trying to smile more.
I'm trying to stop trying.
I'm trying to break down the door and build playgrounds out of cotton,
spend more time moaning, invent prayers
to swallow like rosary beads, holy pills on a string.
I want to choke on something beautiful
and then spit it back up into the mouths of strangers on the street
so I can feel like a good citizen in my community.
I wonder if I have a disease. I don't care if I have a disease.
This is me on a Sunday.

Hello hello I'm a person in the world and I love you.
Hello hello I'm too stupid to say anything about war except
I love that millions of you have died inside me.
Where does all that sperm go?
is a question I am now seriously wondering, my vagina
walls like some sort of graveyard,
except it's never sad. This is the first happy poem
I've ever written about dying, and I don't know
enough about my bank account or refrigerator,
but I have both and today that's enough.

RSVP

This morning I wore heels to the grocery store,
which I mention only because it's something
I've always been too nervous
to do, the way I really wanted to start this poem
with the word BOOM and a glass of vodka, jet
black eyeliner and all the Lycra miniskirts
I like to try on but never buy, the glitter
I've been thinking about whenever
I think about touching your hair and dancing
in your living room, where the heather
evening of a December city filters
through the windows like the smoke
of all the joints I've never lit, all the drugs
I've never done because that also
makes me nervous, like public
transportation, driving in reverse, wearing jewelry, answering
the door/phone, walking into a room, and everything
about shrimp. I'd skydive a hundred times
before getting a flu shot
or pregnant again. I'd skydive
forever if it meant something
to you, if it meant that mountains
meant it when they touched the sky, that the sky
really meant to be so blue.

This Morning the Dew on the Grass Was so Beautiful

it made me want to write a love poem, so I could say something
about being nervous under the pink sky
of your breath, about running barefoot through the fields of the neon summer
that is you when you laugh, which I wish
could be you all the time because when I think
about you crying it feels like all the trees in the world
are turning into oceans. And I wanted to say something
about the universe inside you that I'd like
to be a part of, a place where all the beds are queen-
sized and covered in bright cotton sheets, where hazy
blond mornings stretch their limbs like sleepy wild cats far
past noon and into the purple
dust of the evening that is you walking
down the street, you ordering a sandwich, a drink, you dreaming
on the train while the cityscape climbs over
the horizon and into the sky, which your brain
has always been wider than, even
on the day you were born, which was the day
the stars shone brighter and the Amazon
River bloomed with exotic new fish and the moon
was never so full. But I am missing the freckles, the scars, the shape
of your hands, what you like for breakfast and the food
you hate most. I am missing
the yawn of you, the stretch and the tremble, the sorrow

that lives in your pockets and all the words
you mumble in your sleep. Or maybe
you don't even mumble, you,
who could be anyone, you
are that color I can sometimes taste
but have never seen, the one that exists only
in some ethereal fragment of my amygdala, floating
along the outer edge of my upper right periphery, something
like sapphire and jade but also hot pink and misty
fever grey, like the wings of a bird from the future, where finally
you'll find me and step into the space in my heart I've been carving for you all
these long years.

Daisies the Size of Moons

I was going to tell you that I am the nicest girl
you will ever meet, that in my hair
there are daisies the size of moons, but then I started thinking
about lightning bolts flashing across the nape
of my neck, and I got very scared, because I didn't know
they were there. This was supposed to be
more pleasant. I was going
to invite you for a tea party and read poems
to you in the grassy field behind the hill
that I live in. I was going to wear yellow.
You were going to wear suspenders
and lay back and cross your arms
behind your head. You were going to smile
as you listened to my voice and the birds
in the trees, and I wasn't going to compare
the birds to anything. I was going to let them
be birds, singing and flying
through the bright blue sky we were going
to be under. But then I was feeling so happy that I forgot
to hold on and my mind
slipped like a china cup from between
my fingers, and in that small window
the birds, of course, flew in, and now their wings
are beating against the backs of my eyes

so that I'm tearing up and getting mascara
all over my yellow dress, your white
button-up shirt that you look so nice in. I'm not sure
what this means. I'm not sure why I have such a hard time
keeping things simple. All I wanted
was to write a love poem, a valley in Switzerland, a mouthful
of milk and honey. I wanted to hold your hand
in an English garden humming with swollen pink roses and forest
green ivy, Shakespeare's
eternal summer, thick and golden with a slight breeze from the south
kissing your temples the way I would kiss them
until you died, and even after you died
I would keep my mouth on you until you disappeared completely
because I'm simple like that and have nowhere
else to be. And really everything I've ever wanted
has been so simple, so
lovely, like lace curtains in the front window, dried lavender
in a glass jar next to my bed, over-sized sweaters
from the 1980s that I can buy for five dollars
at the thrift store. I could spend all day
thinking about colors like cranberry and ivory, the warm bath
they pour over my brain when they lie down next to each other
like two people who fell in love 50 years ago
and are still falling. I could spend all winter watching the snow fall, letting candle wax
slowly drip onto my wrists and thinking about how I'll marry
the next man who whispers French in my ear, even though

I won't know what he's saying, I would love him
forever, I am so stupid
and simple like that, there are feathers
coming out of my ears and falling
down around us. I want to put one on your tongue, make you choke
a little, make you taste me. O simple love,
I want to wear sweatpants in your living room
as much as some people want to kill each other, the way some people long to die.

Crush

Today I'm not crushing on you. Handfuls of blue sky
spill out of my pockets and I let them, leaving a trail
of my thoughts about you like bread
for the birds, though I can't decide
if this poem is a fairy tale. Of course I want to be
a goddamn princess, a wreath of violets
braided like your fingers in my hair, wear a bodice
laced so tight it'll bruise my ribs and make me look
even thinner than I am, but also I'd like to tear off this dress and go
crashing through the muddy field I've recently made of my life, to roll
in the shit-yard of my mistakes like the pig
that I am, because there's got to be
something humbling about that, something to ground me, like crying
while looking at yourself in the mirror, or thinking
about your own funeral, the flowers and the songs, all the people
who loved you, their quiet
voices like shadows touching each other on the shoulder
with a tenderness so frail it could crumble any moment even
right here right now if I don't stop thinking
about it. And now I've stopped not thinking
about you because I'd like to love you
with a tenderness like that. I want you to tremble
like a bright dying leaf between my fingers, how I could crush you
at any moment, like the glass between my teeth as I pick up

these pieces of you I've so carelessly dropped and try
to put the sky back together, climb on top of it, call your name.

Coil

I'm drinking a beer so that I'll be
less nervous to call you, though I swear
I'm a grown woman. I'm wearing high-
waisted jeans and yesterday I went to the gynecologist
and for the first time wasn't self-conscious about the spotlight
on my vagina, about my beautiful
blond doctor spreading my poorly-shaven legs, and I felt
so healthy, with her plastic
speculum and fingers inside me, though of course I couldn't help
but compare her fingers to yours, which of course
made me miss you even more, and I wondered if she could tell
that I've been craving you all week, that my cervix
has been feeling like a rosebud raving
on ecstasy, that probably my body
wants to grow your baby inside it. When I think about this
there's a voice that tells me
I'm ridiculous, and I feel a rope trying
to pull me away from you and into
some green suburban lawn in the 1950s, some story
in which you don't appear, some husband
in a suit you'd never wear, and I wonder
why I can't grab a pair of scissors and cut
that rope and let the voice go
like a balloon into the sky, let it explode

and disappear forever, so then I'd only have
this other voice to listen to, the golden one that pulls me
to your bed in the morning, where I'd wear
your favorite T-shirt, fuck you
awake and then two more times
before noon, bite your lip
until it bleeds, let you photograph me
as I put on my underwear, make coffee, sit cross-legged
on your floor, dirty
messy hair, queen
of your smile for the weekend. But sometimes I'm tired
of this voice too, of pulling myself
apart at the seams, always dripping
sticky with honey. And it makes me nervous
that I am so nervous to call you, afraid that it means
we're not as close to something
as I'd like us to be, or that I'm not as mature
as I think I am, but wouldn't it be worse
if you didn't shake me, make me sweat, if I didn't
feel like you could crush me
into a fine white powder you could rub
on your gums? I think it's a good thing
that I can't think about you without feeling
like a cat sliding up against some cosmic
wall, some vibrating magnetic field that twists my spine
the way a clown makes animal
balloons at a birthday party, and I thought

this beer would help unwind me
a little, at least enough to call you
and say Hi, but it's only making
me coil even tighter, and I've decided to wait
until tomorrow to call you
because right now just thinking about you and me being
alive at the same time is making me so happy
and nervous, so much that I'm forgetting
the voices or what I came here
to do, and I keep thinking
about growing your baby, about you
inside me last week, which makes me feel
like there's a tiny giraffe licking
the salt from the small of my back,
and the thing I love most about you
is that you'd say I'd be a fool
not to drop everything and let him have me till dawn.

November

Tonight the wind is a white devil, scraping
his teeth against our skin. The trees can't promise me anything,
and I wish I could say I don't need any promises.
I wish I could eat six small meals a day and go to church once a week, wear a cross
around my neck and spend my days putting flowers in the windows of homeless shelters.
I want to be your homeless shelter, grow a vegetable garden and
make the shooting stop. Is it so terrible
to want people to love each other more?
Nights like this I love everyone but myself and wonder which pill
would let me into my own heart. I just want to rest, to stop
under the sky and feel its blue drip down into my throat like
some futuristic honey from God's everlasting mouth.
I've spent the last six months building a field
of light to tuck my bones inside of but
lately the light isn't enough. Lately it's been getting dark at five
and my brother is a veteran of war. I keep brushing my teeth but
my mother is still lonely and all I want
is to bake a fucking meatloaf and stop
thinking about the fact that your body
won't always be a body, that you won't always be.
I'm picturing your hands in a jar next to my bed and it's not
that I don't believe in heaven but that I'd rather

go on touching you forever. Fuck the church. I want to reincarnate as the tree
that someone carves into your coffin so I can hold
your bones as they crumble into the star
dust they came from, the space that mouthed you.

All the Birthday Candles

December 10th is Emily Dickinson's birthday
and also mine. I tell people this
as if it means something. As if sharing a birthday
makes us friends, allies
across time, like two leaves grown on the same tree
just over a century apart, or gate posts
on either side of a field that could be a cemetery
if all the things in it seemed more dead, if their echoes
weren't so loud. I keep hearing
the scrape of the iceberg slicing open
the steel belly of the Titanic, the cries
of children drowning. I think of all the bullets
people have shot at each other
and themselves, and my temples
ache like that time I had a seizure and felt like someone
was banging my head against the bars of a cage underwater, the closest
to someone trying to kill me
I've ever felt. Sometimes my ears ring
and I think it's the vibrations of the atomic
bomb and all the wars
I'm too sensitive to talk about, though someone keeps
projecting war films on the back wall
of my brain, stained sepia clips
of legless soldiers in trenches in France, pyramids

of dead bodies, Anne Frank's toothy grin, smokestacks
that make my nose burn so hard I'm afraid if I sneeze I'll cover
this table in ashes, which will look and feel and smell
no different than my own ashes
someday. Vietnam is a rusty fork
twisting my brain like spaghetti, like the intestines
of a soldier shot in the stomach. Headlines say weekend violence
in southern Afghanistan rose the U.S. death toll
to over 2,000 this year, so I write this down
because I don't know what else to do. It's early October
and Jeff has been dead for half a year. I hate
that in all my thoughts about him
he is floating horizontally above the county roads I drive on
in the early mornings, a shadow
between the trees like Olympian torches, the trees like burning towers,
like all the birthday candles he'll never blow out. I'm always reaching
back through time, brushing snow
off of headstones, reaching
for Emily's hands. I want to bake a cake
with her, have a birthday party
in the snow. I want to lace my fingers in hers
and hold the world that's come between us
like an orphan in our arms, like a child
whose parents died in a fire
no one knows how to put out. I want to sing
to it, tell it to make a wish, let it believe, for a moment,
in something greater than itself.

If This Were a Protest My Sign Would Be Blank

I've been eating way too much chocolate
these past few days, which really fucks up
my bikini-season diet, which is really
a ridiculous thing to waste time thinking about
because regardless of my pant size
one day I'm going to die. This is not a newsflash
but every time I think about it, it's as if I'm being beat
in the stomach with a baseball bat, and on it are the signatures
of everyone I've ever loved. It's amazing
that I continue to recover from these assaults, that somehow
I get out of bed. I make coffee. Every day
I brush my teeth. I smooth Burt's Bees chapstick
on my lips, which are filled with blood, and how incredible
is that? How incredible, that I'm able to stand up
and put one foot in front of the other, shuffle forward one
small miracle at a time. How incredible, yet how
pathetic, as I sit here with my coffee and my diet,
while nearly 2,000 miles away
my little brother is marching in the 5 a.m. rain with the rest
of his infantry platoon, training for war, stripping
his civilian self like it's the worst habit in the world. And I'm not sure
what to tell you about war. I'm not sure
what any of these guns mean or
why. I'm not sure, Mr. President. I'm

not sure, Lady Liberty. If this were a protest
my sign would be blank. If this were a protest, I'd ask
my brother for a bullet so I could suck
on it, get real close to death, give me
a life lesson, turn my insides into metal
instead of snail guts. I am
so soft, some days
I forget how to walk, my knees
about to collapse under all this
imaginary weight, while my brother
skydives into this life as if it's been waiting for him
all these billions of years. *You just keep going,*
he says. *You're not going to die*
from running too much. I think about him
hiking 25 miles in the desert with 60 pounds on his back, knowing
that one wrong step could set off a bomb
that would blow him to pieces, that he could
be stabbed in the neck by a four-year-old
asking for candy.
I think about my four-year-old
asking for candy, how happy she is, not stabbing
anyone in the neck, how right now
my brother still has a neck and it holds
up his head and inside his head
there are thoughts and dreams that move
through him like wind across the desert, blowing
some dust around another goddamn day.

While I'm Busy

It's embarrassing, how many people died today
and how much I still want
to kiss you in Paris, San Francisco, your bed
in August with the windows open, where my tongue has gone sore
from sucking itself, and I feel
like an ice-cream cone someone dropped
on the sidewalk in July, like you could drink
my pink hips though a straw, so I've been working
on my darkness, but lipstick
looks stupid on me, and maybe I need to spend more time
reading history books or watching
the news, but ever since you touched my thigh I can't stop thinking
about rubbing the inside of a daisy
on your arms in the spring, staining your skin
gold with pollen while you tell me
about your father, a dream in which you were sailing
in a small boat by yourself, and I could hold your hand and drift
away from all the war going on inside me, and I mean
the actual war, where right now my brother
is wearing an actual uniform, holding
an actual gun, and maybe by now he's actually
killed someone, which puts a bullet in my throat, the killing and all the leaves
I imagine tearing apart inside him, and sometimes I feel like the sun
when I kiss you, like a really

big bitch, shining obnoxiously on all those rows
of graves like teeth, when I spend all morning
burying my nose in that mossy space between your thigh
and groin, while my brother
is digging for bombs in the sand, trying not
to blow himself to pieces, while I'm busy peeling
your coarse hair from my lips, and he
hears children screaming, but someone has got to
remember to let morning in through the blinds, let it slice
our bodies into delicate shapes
of light and dark to put in each others'
mouths like fruit, be the fruit, smash
a strawberry against my throat, come inside me, don't let all those kids
on the front line die for nothing.

Birth Poem

Because I've given birth I feel obligated
to write a poem about giving birth, to draw you
some elaborate metaphor so that you, too,
can relive the hot blood, the fucking
pain, the six-inch needle in the spine, the catheter, the monitors,
the almost-C-section, the insensitive nurses, the soft
and sticky top of the fetus head crowning
between your legs like the queen of your body
she has been. And you don't even scream but somehow
she escapes you, after which she is no longer a queen but a creature
with a lolling head and shrill limbs attached to a rib cage
not even a hummingbird could fit inside of.
The nurses take her to the other side of the room
while the doctor pushes on your abdomen and extracts
your placenta, which looks like what the organs
of someone who died in a car accident must look like,
which is something you don't think of until later
because you're too busy watching as they clean her,
suction the slime out of her throat and nose,
measure her, weigh her, label her, slide
a hat over her mushy skull and wrap her
in a white blanket, at last placing her in your arms like
a tiny cloud. And you try to grasp the fact that this body
came from inside of your body, which came from inside

of your mother's body, and thinking about this
is like trying to imagine the beginning of time or what's on the other side
of the universe, and your brain feels like a black
hole, the way it threatens to swallow you, and in this core
of the human experience you've never felt more alien, more broken, more
mortal, and you and your daughter make eye contact
for the first time, while somewhere a storm
tears down a house, a woman plants a garden, a man
gasps on life support while you
and your daughter stare at each other as if to say *Who are you and what
have you done to me?*

Smoke

Yesterday I bought a pack of cigarettes,
even though I should save all my money and even though
I don't usually smoke, the other day
I wanted to die and knew I had
to do something. I kept thinking
about Sylvia Plath's children and the rocks
in Virginia Woolf's pockets, about razors
and bathtubs, ribbons of blood
moving like smoke through the water, about Anne
Sexton's starry night and lightning
cracking my spine like a tree in a summer storm, about drowning
or freezing to death, my lungs burning and brain
swelling like a bruise, exploding
under the pressure of all my dirty oxygen, how with a soft
pop it would go dark, like a bulb
burning out, a final
small kiss, and I wanted to say something else here,
about a gun or something
violent like that, but I'm looking at these words
I just put on the page, and feel the sudden need
to go shave my legs, which are very
hairy because it's winter and it's not like I have
a home to invite someone over to, or someone
I'd want to invite, which is kind of

a lie, which means I'm hiding
something, which means there is something
to hide, something to find, something
inside me, a reason
to keep digging my nails into my skin, scrambling
up the dirt wall of myself, from the bottom
of the grave I thought I had
no choice but to throw
myself into, where I might be right now if it weren't
for my cigarettes, this buzz, this sudden
ache between my legs when I blow
the smoke between my lips, light some candles, run
a fresh blade up my thigh, think of his mouth.

Down into the Grass

It makes me sad that most of the men
I'd like to fuck are dead. And I don't even want
to fuck my ex but last night dreamed
that I did, and woke up feeling sad, feeling
fat because all the pizza
I ate yesterday, and I can't help but wonder
if there's a malfunction inside me, some switch
I forgot to turn on, or if there even
is a switch, if I'll always
be fumbling along the cool dirt walls
of a cave, holding a white candle, thinking
about my friends, how much I love them and how much I wish
this love was enough, this green field, this gold sun, this
big sky love. I wish I was typing this
on a typewriter in the sky, or under it, I mean, that my hair
was straight and blond for a day, my nose
a little smaller, that I wouldn't have to
plug in so many things
before I could use them. I think what I'm saying
is that I'm confused. And how couldn't
I be, with all this hair on my legs, all this snow melting and talk
about guns? I want to know what it's like
to live in a place I feel comfortable
living in, to say this town

is my town, and I live here, and wouldn't you like
to come over for dinner? I keep thinking
about you coming over for dinner, looking at all
the books on my living room shelf, asking
what you can help with, since I know
you would ask, standing
in my kitchen in your bright green socks. I want to know
how those women on the porch in Montpelier
got to be so happy, drinking wine on a summer
afternoon without men, laughing
the way only women
can laugh with other women, a flock of birds
erupting from them over
and over again, how even the birds are laughing, their wings like arrows
pointing in every direction
except for back at themselves. But of course I am always
pointing back at myself, always so
concerned with what I'm doing or not
doing enough of, and this is getting
so existential, I'm so uncomfortable, it's after 1 p.m.
and I'm still in pajamas, riding a horse
I wish was wilder, would buck me off,
and send me flailing, rudely, would hurt me, wake me
up from this stupid dream about love
and silverware, Italian
dinners in the city and day trips
to the coast in our third

summer, any summer. I want to know
what it's like to stay, to want to stay. It doesn't
really matter what I'm wearing, I just want
to make you hungry. I just want
to be adored. I want to stop
wanting to be adored. I want to stop
stopping myself, slamming my fingers
in this oven door, and so I am going to stop here, on the longest
day of summer, even though you are a man
I'd like to fuck, which makes me
scared that you are dead, I am going to stop here and wear
a light blue dress made of cotton, and wait for you
to lift it like a cloud around my shoulders and push me
down into the grass the way no friend of mine could.

Pretty Head

I know a girl who has everything
I think I want. She cries a lot and it makes me want
to slap her hard across the mouth.
I want to knock her out, slam her pretty
head against a stucco wall
and then resuscitate her, expand her lungs and clear
a space in her brain for us to lie down in.
We wouldn't make a very good couple but still sometimes
I think about marrying her
in a house with high ceilings and crown molding.
Everything we own would be antique so that forever
we'd be young among our things, which would all
be covered in pollen because the windows
would always be open so that
we'd feel tempted to jump and turn
to each other with kindness. I can't even paint
my nails without thinking about her.
I want to ask her which color
I should use on my toes. I bet my toes
are prettier than hers, though her knees
are probably bonier and I can't
stop thinking about how much I'd like to slide
my fingers behind them as she curls
like a fawn into the grass when she thinks no one is looking.

But I am always looking. Always trying to sip the
champagne from her elbows, pull her into
the sky like a flute, pull her spine apart one
pearly bone at a time. I'd like to hide red velvet petals
between her vertebrae, watch her grind them to dust
as she arches her back into a bridge and stares
at me upside down. I want her to stare at me but she's always
looking at me sideways, as if I have
something she needs and she's plotting
a way to rob me and would kill me if only
she knew what to take. If only I had
something to take, if only I could finger
the gold star she's super-
glued to my forehead, then maybe I could rise
up out of this fire and move towards her
with milk and honey in my mouth, wipe her tears and hold
her hand in mine without wanting
to crush it for being so beautiful and hers.

Unborn

Today you are a universe
I'm not sure exists, and for a while I thought
the mystery was nice, all the
swirls of cosmic dust
always moving through you,
but it's been so long since we've touched
that I'm afraid I made you up,
so I've moved
over to the window
where I can feel the white light from the snow
on my face, because I like the way
it makes me feel clean like
a woman on earth, bathing
in a lake with other women, and for the first time I'm imagining
myself with breasts, full
and round like they were when I was pregnant, floating
to the surface like cream, like the head of a beer, except that you're not
putting your mouth on me
this time, this time
I'm eating, filling
myself from the inside out without thinking
about your cock, about brick walls and digging
my hips into yours in the middle of the night, this time
it's a white-hot noon and these women

have nipples the color of tangerines, like the flesh
of blood oranges, and when they laugh it's from their bellies, and they have bellies,
and I'm trying so hard
to have a belly
and lean against a tree
in the shade with these women, smoking clove cigarettes, pulling
out grass with my toes, for the first time
I want to be bigger than I am, thick like a mango, I want sex
to be meaningless, to eat salmon from the lake
where I bathed with these women, to eat with these women, with my fingers, when I think
about touching these women it's like touching
myself while at the same time trailing
a finger along the curve
of the moon as it wanes, and it wanes, and I feel like a sweater
I've pulled over my head, breathing
against my own mouth, with these women, my arms like vines, my lips
stained dark because I've been drinking
wine, been watching the sky
slip into dusk, been trying so hard
to keep the white light from fading, as the women
slip into a dream I once had, a painting I made, and yet here I am
with your shadows on my face, fading
into my skinny purple self
again, moving back to the couch, my legs curled
underneath me, like a fawn, pulling

the sweater off completely, naked without you, and how I wish
we had something to break, that we could make a bloody mess
on our tiled kitchen floor, that we had
a kitchen floor that we called ours, so that instead of swimming
in the cosmos like a tangled web
of something unborn, something yet to come, this
could be the break-up, a birth scene, and I could escape from you screaming, escape
from you, finally, taste you
from the inside out, say
I've been inside you, I've known you, life is tearing
us apart at the seams, you're hurting me, I'm hurting you, now push and let me go.

Professionals

It's Sunday morning and I'm in the dark
theater of myself again, waiting for the next
movie to start, this Technicolor
film from the '60s, something with lawn chairs
and cigarettes, beautiful
women in their late 30s wearing red
and white bathing suits, lounging like cats, untouchable, freckles
like leopard spots kiss their hot shoulders. I want to stand
under the blazing summer sky with one hand
on my hip. For weeks I've been posing
in front of the mirror like this, trying
to be more of a cunt, but I'm stuck
with this girlish frame, wearing pink pajamas, having
a slumber party with my girlfriends, my girlfriends, I'm always thinking
about my girlfriends, how far they've carried me
on what feels like a white sofa
with a silk canopy, because I am so tired
of spending my days
without you, sometimes I just need
to rest like an infant in the shade. It scares me,
how hard it is to live, how easily
my body breathes, how that I really
would have your baby if you asked. My breasts
tingle at the thought of it, and I wonder if this

has something to do with Jesus. I would like
to be saved. I would like to fall
into the arms of paramedics, like I did when I was pregnant
and had a seizure in the arms
of the only man who's ever loved me, the home
I made and then left. I would like
to plead insanity, wear white and surrender
myself to professionals, cool, aloof, like the women
in my head, those long-
limbed gods sweating on the lawn, having a Coke, absentmindedly
brushing their collarbones, shooing flies
away like flies, like men, like flies.

Revolution

Lately whenever someone asks me Where
have you been? I want to say
In love, and then I wonder Who
I am in love with and for
How long I've been there. Do these cigarettes
count? I am not
in love with the boy
poet who lit my cigarette
under the hot lights outside of the
hotel in Boston, but I keep thinking
about the scruff on his jaws, the way
he leaned in like some guy from a movie, how I felt old Holly-
wood sexy, a place people
pay millions to live, like my life
was a movie but I knew it was really
my life, like that time I was driving
on the county road and saw that white llama
standing in the tall grass,
so that the llama looked like it was floating
on a thick green breeze, its face toward the sun,
and inside me I felt
the llama's lips peel into a smile
and I knew the llama was happy the way some people
say they know God, feel his

light guiding them through the dark, which is what
I call kissing
long-limbed boys
whose mouths make you feel like a carnival
ride in July, it's Elizabeth in her gray romper, stretching
like a cat in the half-light she's always
writing me about, the way cotton
candy melts into your tongue as if it's been dying
to taste you, it's tasting you, God I mean, it's
your tongue, reading
an obituary out loud to someone
who is sitting on your bed, it's someone
sitting on your bed, it's having
a bed. My bed has been empty for years and I'm still wondering
who I am in love with. Does everyone
count? I mean that figuratively. I mean that if you're reading this,
probably I love you. I mean that today I'm feeling beautiful, like the llama, it's so easy
to love when you're feeling beautiful, when your insides
are filled with bright fish
that nibble at your wrists
without drawing blood, and what I wonder is not
even why but whose mouth
all these rivers came from, and what's
going to happen
when I wake up feeling ugly, when the rivers
run dry and I wake up with a mouthful of dirt and fish

bones in my hair? But God, fuck
philosophy, the sun is out and I
just want to party. Does my therapist
count? Inside me there's an army
of tiny people with flags, saying something
about a revolution. I told them
about the news report
about the woman
whose boyfriend raped then
killed her infant daughter. I show them photos
of the guts of soldiers
in Vietnam, and dream about my brother, wondering
how many people he's shot, how many
he killed, how many of his friends
died in front of him, how many he saved, and what's the word
for what he feels? for what I feel
when the army inside me doesn't disappear,
not even blowing trumpets, this parade of blue
and green light, moving like a song down my spine and out
through my tail bone
down into the center of the planet, and now I realize
it's the planet I'm in love with, this dirt and my life
sprawling from it like a sea
anemone, and I wonder why I feel
like that's not okay, as if someone
right now wants to slap me
for ending this poem with the one

thing we claim we're always searching for, and I don't mean
some metaphorical light but just that
this morning I woke up again in a bed.

Everything Beautiful Happens in My Mouth

And it's March and every day
the earth leans toward the sun
a little more, like someone at a party, uncrossing and crossing
her legs, shifting her weight from her right hip
to her left to be closer
to the man on her left, his laughter and his smell, even though
he doesn't really smell
like anything, she can sense
something pulling her close to him, something like a bird
happening in the back of her throat when he laughs, when he moves
to reach for his drink. And every day
I hear birds again, and I feel like I'm hearing them
for the first time since it snowed,
but I don't know for sure
because birds aren't something
I pay much attention to, unless I'm anxious for spring,
and listening. I've gained four pounds in the last two weeks,
which is probably a sign of spring, since hunger
is the body's sign of hope. I painted my toenails pink and keep thinking
about cherry blossoms and dogwoods, thick
sweet petals spilling out of my mouth, because everything
beautiful happens in my mouth, which might explain why
I brush my teeth and tongue
so much, always sweeping

the stage, like a Zamboni I'm clearing
the arena for love. It's almost spring and I'm falling
in love with no one, but falling
all the same, putting flowers in my tea and thinking about all the cerulean
afternoons we haven't spent together, barefoot in the clover, the clouds
pulling our hands into the air, rolling our shoulders
down and back into the grass
like a train slowing down because it's tired
of being a train, the rush and the burning, the hollow
midnight whistle. I don't want
to rush anywhere
with anyone. I want to wear cotton underwear
that covers my ass, a white T-shirt with a pocket on the front
and cut-off denim shorts that are one size too big. I want my red hair
to be the only fiery
thing about you. I want to sleep in a bed
next to a man who won't dream of me all night, a man who
doesn't need me, who reaches
behind him and pulls me up against his back without thinking
about it, without even wanting to, the way right now
the snow outside couldn't stop melting in streams down the driveway
even if it tried, and it doesn't try, and in a few weeks the flowers
won't try to bloom, they won't
even know they are flowers, but they'll rise up all the same,
and be beautiful, their soft mouths hanging open, like my daughter
when she was one and pointed
at the moon every night there was a moon, the well

of awe inside her, the light we were born with, the natural
order of things, I want you
to spend your days moving toward me without ever knowing why.

Red Paper Heart

When I think about my childhood there are a dozen
cameramen rushing
around the field in the back
of my brain, trying to locate
a single place, a mountain, a back yard,
a living room for this story
to call home. There is a dog
my brother used to read stories to and a cat
I named Tiger and loved almost
as much as I loved the boy who lived across the street
when we lived in Kentucky, the boy from Hawaii
with hair as unruly as mine, who wrote *Love*
on a red paper heart and gave it to me
for Valentine's Day in fifth grade, how I slept
with that heart under my pillow
for a year, fingered
the ink and the edges
his hands had once touched, wrote *I love Kyle*
on the mirror after the shower, which I forgot
to erase, so when my dad took a shower
he saw what I'd written
and got mad and told me
I was too young
to know what love is, and now I'm thinking

I should have asked him if he knew
what love is, what burning
ever engulfed him, if a creature
had ever tapped the maple from his spine, filled his belly
with a feeling like lava, like at any moment
his hips might melt together, collapse, and then spread
into flame, a new sun for planets
to spin themselves
into life around, a hot bright cry
against the cold death
he must have breathed so much of
as a soldier in Saudi Arabia the same year
my brother was born. And this war must be
one of the reasons we don't talk
about feelings, why I would never tell him that the moon
always makes me feel naked enough
to cry, that I like to imagine a blue thread of light
keeping my spine from collapsing
into a pile of dust in the pit of my pelvis when I think
about anybody dying, that there are needles
I've been sucking from the mouth
of a boy in the snow in an effort
to stitch myself together, that there is no such thing
as myself and
together, or a place I call home, or a love
that has anything to do with knowing.

Big Spoon I Keep Wetting My Lips Against

I hope you feel beautiful today, drive west
with your daughter,
and take photos of mountains. I have a daughter but this is not
a note to myself. This is
so far from what I wanted and I'm not
even wearing mascara today. My eyes are swollen
today. I want to celebrate today, which scares me, because I'm in the same
damn town again, floating on a cloud that might open
at any moment, empty me like a bag
of bones into the mud. I've caught the eyes
of three strangers today, and I must look happy, because each
of them smiled at me, as if
they were returning something, reflecting
some light, some
new season. I want to call this
the season of women, the season of hair, and dirt
beneath my nails. I'm obsessed
with our bodies, the curve of our spines like a great
big spoon I keep
wetting my lips against, thinking
about holy water and waiting
for the darkness inside me
to flare up again, the smoke in the sky, the dull
ache for his mouth. The ache to run. I'm waiting

for foreign cities to call me
again, their buildings like fingers, I'm waiting
for a knuckle to make
its gentle way between my teeth, for desire
to gut me with its jagged knife, pull out my intestines and unwind
them, make me follow my own
bloody mess across the country. I'm waiting and nothing
is happening. I am so calm. It's not going
to last but maybe I've finally
reached some frontier, like a pioneer I am building
my home here in April, my home in the sky, my home
without a bed or even
a door. It's sort of amazing
that I've come this far and haven't died, that I have
an eye appointment today, that my daughter
is at preschool and I'm not
hating my life in a cubicle, a marriage, or under
a bridge. I'm writing a poem in a coffee shop but might as well
be topless in the sun, my small breasts even
smaller, flatter, as I cross my arms behind my head and spread
myself beneath the sky, on a lonely
road in North Dakota. I want to be flat like that, open
like that. I'm not eating
fresh fish in California and I'm
not hungry. I am your daughter and we
are driving west. We
are driving home without a car, without

even driving, we
are going nowhere, and I hope you feel
beautiful today, smash your crown to pieces, give
away your life and in the morning it will crawl back, kiss your fingers, make
you queen.

American Spirit

I'm really no different than a caterpillar
is something I thought today
while sitting outside of my parents' house, smoking
a cigarette they wouldn't approve of. I was never
a rebellious teenager, and now I feel dumb
for feeling so cool
with this slender burning between my fingers, the small
voice inside that says *You*
are 25 and not allowed
to feel dumb and cool anymore.
I've spent most of my life
trying to be better than myself, like a horse
always squeezing her eyes
together, trying to grow
a big sparkly horn, some flag that says *Look*
at me I'm special. But I'm not special and what
a relief it is to just sit here with this cigarette like a normal
person, thinking about the slender
hips of the boy I've been kissing, sweet
and hard like the bark of vanilla, the sort of boy you
love only in the summer when every-
thing is swollen and you're
not sad enough to need him all the time, when the sky
is a balloon that blows

itself up inside you each morning so that you
spend most of every day
with your head thrown back like an open-
mouthed maniac, laughter spilling from your throat like
a vodka-soaked swarm of
bumblebees and violets, and I know
it's dangerous
to be so fucking sweet, to kiss boys
who have girlfriends and feelings, to have feelings, to lie
in the sun for so long that my bones
forget they are bones, to forget about cancer
and imagine the marrow
flowing through my fingers like golden
lava, my blood like a dream, like I'm not
really real and
how happy I am.

Moon Dog

There is nothing extraordinary about my life,
which is something I just now realized
smoking a cigarette
outside on Laura's patio
where last spring she hung round paper lanterns,
a string of hollowed out moons
blowing in the wind, which is how
I've been feeling, hollowed
out, kicked out, locked
out from some secret
I imagine is buzzing
in the Christmas lights people
keep plugging in even though
it's February and I am sleeping
on an air mattress in Laura's living room,
stuffing my clean laundry
into my dirty suitcase,
my suitcase that my mother used
when she went to Germany last summer
where I was born
in a hospital
like most people. Like most people
I get lonely. Like most people I think
about sex a lot

though maybe unlike most people
I don't like to be touched
all that much, unless the feeling
is extraordinary, and I'm trying to decide
what I mean by extraordinary, though it's not
a decision as much as it is
a pearlescent object lodged under
the skin of my breast bone, something
I keep trying to finger like braille, like a plate
with hand-painted gold and pink flowers, something
a Persian cat might lick
milk out of, that might break
if you held it.
I think it's extraordinary
if you say you don't
want to be adored, and like most people
I want to be special, which makes me
so normal, just another handful
of carbon and oxygen trying to spin
its dusty self into a planet, someone's home, something
a moon might like to pull close now and then.

And when I am born, I become free. That is the foundation of my tragedy.

—Clarice Lispector

To a Real Party

I spend half of every day recovering from the parties
I'm always throwing, all the celebration
and mourning inside me. I am one of the happiest
and saddest people you will ever meet, which is why I like to go outside
and photograph people doing things like laughing and
looking at each other. Right now I'd like to look at someone,
and also the stars. I'd like to put on purple jeans
and walk through the snow, go to a real party, have a beer
with a friend and stake a white flag
into the soft pink earth of my brain.
I like to think about earth
from the perspective of an astronaut
in outer space. I will always be amazed
at how round and perfect we are, never crashing
into the moon or sun, each hour
unfolding so reliably. If one day I wake up
and the sun doesn't rise,
I won't be surprised. I'm actually surprised
that every day it does rise, that the earth
hasn't broken its axis in two, tired
from carrying us through the salty dark, heavy
with all the people we've buried inside of it. And it's sort of nice
to think of earth this way, at least for a moment, to look at us
from a distance, and I mean all of us, the dead

and the living, the ashes and the bones, how we're all stuck here
together in the end, no matter how hard we might try
to throw ourselves off, and so there's no reason
not to worship each other like a field of poppies
opening their mouths to the sun, to drown ourselves deep
in the red mouth of love. When I was little I would cry myself to sleep
because I couldn't stop thinking about that commercial
with the starving children in Africa, their small faces
already aged by sorrow and swarming
with flies, their swollen bellies like funeral balloons
hanging from their tender spines. Then I fell in love
with one boy after another, held their hands, and felt like a Christmas tree
surrounded by a family in red flannel
pajamas, unwrapping white lights
and vintage gold ornaments, hot chocolate
steaming on the stove. And I decided we should always
be in love with someone, even if they don't
love us back, even if we end up feeling like a Christmas tree
in a wood chipper, which is how part of me
always feels, which is why I make sure
to eat lots of snowflakes and let my mouth break
into a wave of silver light, a halo
for the head of every child, a handful of glitter
I will glue to your face only to spend
the rest of my life licking it off, sweetening the world
so I can bear to swallow.

This Is What It's like to Fall out of Love

I used to write poems about how the small of my back
must feel in your hands—like china, the delicate bone, white
curve and arc. About how when your hair fell into your eyes it was like snow
falling softly on the pines outside your window. But then the snow turned
 into rain, the god-
damn unpredictable weather, and all the ink bled into blue
and black veins, the pages breaking like, breaking like
waves, and I began falling like, falling
like something terrible I stumbled out of the wake of you, away
from the shore of you, disentangled
myself from your thighs, your mouth
has left bruises on the insides of my elbows, they look
like little violets, they're so beautiful, it hurts now to think about everything
 and I
am lonelier than pills in a sock drawer, the mattress
that committed suicide on the highway.

Rain Poem

Because I left you I've been sleeping
on couches, in my brother's bed, on the futon
in my parents' study, where a nail is sticking
out of the wall because last night I took down the clock
because its tick-tock was making me nervous, making me think
about green muddy graveyards, and I felt
like a pebble on a mountain, a small
terrible avalanche, plummeting towards some darkness, some bottom, some
grave someone had already dug for me, even though
I want my body burned when I die, my ashes scattered
over an ocean I've never been in, and even though
I tried to think about the passing of time
as the healer that it is, about our daughter
growing old enough to understand love
and how sometimes people fall out of it, for her to go to school
and have friends who make her happy on the days
that I've failed her, which lately feels
like every day, every
fucking minute, and even though
I tried to ignore the clock, tried to drift
into a dream in which everything was light bending
in waves of watercolor blue and someone
was holding me, breathing
into my hair, still,

the clock kept slipping
its needles into my skin, and I started
to hyperventilate, like I do
whenever I think about needles, like I did
when the nurse drew my blood when I was pregnant and you drove three
  hours
just to hold my hand and tell me I looked beautiful
even though I felt
like a bloated alien with a warping spine, defying gravity
just to hold the planet spinning out from above my hips, to feed
the tiny alien inside,
and so the clock
had to go,
and then it was quiet,
and I pretended that time had stopped
so I could imagine myself, for the moment,
suspended in the dark like
a star whose light has stopped emptying out of it, for the moment, I pretended
that maybe time was ticking backwards, back
to the night we slept in the bed
of your pickup truck, the pines
all lit up in the moonlight, your eyes
still copper moons I wanted to lie down inside of, your face
still something I wanted to die holding,
your hands still like water, the way they cleaned me, pulled
me under and how I never wanted to come back up, back
to us standing in the headlights in the fog in the rain that warm

November evening, how we stepped into each other for the first time, how
our mouths
moved against each other as if they'd been moving toward each other
since the first threads of DNA in our lips wove themselves together, back
to before you loved me, before
you knew me, before the night
you pressed me up against the back of the house and I made you promise
you wouldn't leave me.

The Soft Dark

Tonight my brother's friend
has been dead for three months,
and I think I might give up talking.
I can never seem to say
what I really mean to say. And why
do we expect the mouth, that small
sliver of our bodies, to do all
the talking, when we have
so many other parts? I wonder
what the earth has done to Jeff
and his parts, shrinking
inside that pressed midnight blue uniform,
his big hands now frail inside
those crisp white gloves.
How much muscle is left?
And what happens to the eyes? Those bright
winter blue eyes, how they danced inside his head
when he laughed, like twin planets
breathing close to the sun, like suns
themselves, the center
of youth, boyhood, plastic
toy soldiers, and summers in the pool.
But tonight there is just this planet,
this earth, orbiting

alone in the dark, like each of us
in the end. At a party the music
is loud for a reason. These beautiful
faces in the soft dark say all
I need to hear, and when I dance
I'm telling the whole room secrets
I didn't know I had, though sometimes
even my body fails me, like tonight
my head, heavy, like a bear
storing fat, getting ready to sleep
for months, because the year has worn it out.
If I make eye contact with one
more person, I'm afraid the tower
of good things I've built inside me
will crumble under the lovely weight
of itself, and so for now
I'm just going to sit here, alone,
and think, and what I'm thinking
is that instead of praying, people
should spend more time touching
themselves between the legs,
and maybe then
God would answer,
and maybe then
I wouldn't have had to stand
before Jeff's open casket, fumbling
for words to say to his younger sister

as she squeezes her dead brother's hand
and says "Doesn't he look great?"
Maybe then I wouldn't have had to throw
my arms around her, pull her head
into my chest like the child
she is, and think about how there are more cells
in my body than stars
in the sky, yet there's nothing
I could do with any of them
to hold up the night
falling down around us
like the ash from the cigarettes
of those young men
on the corner down the street.
I think I am going to go out
and walk past them now,
and instead of saying hello I'm going
to slide my hands around the slender
waist and down into the front pockets
of the dark-haired one in the red, just
for a moment. That is all
I want to say.

The Smaller I Become in It

People keep telling me I look so skinny,
and although they say it as an observation, I take it
as a compliment, like a medal
made of orchids that I can pin to my chest, like a creamy
silk dress to drape
myself in, to drip with, I take it
like a Pulitzer Prize, like I've done something
worth doing, I take a small sip of wine
and dance in my underwear
alone in my room, feeling
as if there are sunrays
beaming from my armpits and the ridges
of my ribs, my light touching everyone
I know, falling more in love
with the world the smaller
I become in it, though most days
I'm not actually touching anyone,
because actually touching most people
requires all the effort
it takes me to breathe for a day,
and probably most people
won't find me beautiful
really, not in that wholesome
curvy honey way, not like a stallion or arctic

wolf, but more like a spider
people study in awe, like an accident
on the side of the road you have to
slow down and watch, to see if there are stretchers,
white sheets or blood, if body
parts are hanging
out of windows, if anyone's standing
with their face in their hands, having
a worse day than you, and if I get any thinner
people will start to look at me
and feel sad, and I'll take it
like a martyr, like a lover, I'll let you stare at me, say yes,
I'm a wreck, yes, I know suffering, yes, I am dying too.

American Mouth

I'm in the coffee shop thinking about death
again, how with every second I am moving closer to her bed and yet with every
thought I have I am moving
deeper inside my life, another brick, another feather, another word
added onto this house I am building,
so that one day I can live in it or something. I don't know. Maybe it's a mountain
I am thinking of, something to stand on top of and breathe.
Something for people to point at
when I'm dead. But I don't want
to turn my life into a metaphor about an accidental rock in the sky. I came here
to talk about death, how it's strange that I don't believe
in life after it, even though year after year
Spring rises from her frozen grave like
some bride of Christ, green ghost with flowers in her hair, cool fingers
brushing your forehead as you lie back in the new
grass and wait for the sun
to pull you up out of yourself. At least that's what I
do, always waiting, always moping
in some dark room, kicking at rocks with my dirty Converse, feeling too ugly
to talk to anyone, until I think about the world
and all the kids

who will die today, murdered in the street by a government
made up of humans, killed by their parents, people with hands
just like mine, which makes me feel both awful
and okay, thankful and guilty, my pretty American mouth full of baby's
breath while real babies get the breath
shaken out of them by people who have to
somehow be different than I am, more angry, more fucked up, more sad, but still
American, how tomorrow we'll still
get dressed up and go to the movies, we'll still
eat popcorn and laugh, and more people will die, and we'll get married all the same, dancing
in orchards and touching each other while the sky turns to blood but
we won't think of it like that.

All the Birds from the Trees

Outside it's snowing and I'm trying
to feel clean. These are the last hours
of the first quarter-century of my life
and I want to spend them stripping
the silver from my veins and all this cybernetic energy
I don't know what to do with. Was it in me
when I was born, did I scrape it
from the walls of my mother as I slid down inside her, gathering something
to hold on to as I broke into the world?
I keep hearing stories about the trees in people's childhoods,
the dogwood and the peach tree, the willow by the pond,
and I wish time was a pool I could dip my hand into
because there's something between me
and my brother when we were kids
that I'd like to put under my pillow tonight, some marigold
cloud I need to lie down on for a while, let it carry me
until I find whatever light I need
to press against the backs of my knees while my brother boards the plane
for Afghanistan this Friday. I keep wanting
to press my ribs against his ribs, move his fingers
in a circle in the snow, and cut out the pearl
in his chest so I can save it in a jar
for the next nine months, have some moonlight to wash him with
when he comes back. I keep wanting to clean

this war from our lives, which is like trying to stop
our blood from being red, this black
steel bell in my chest from banging
against my lungs, and because I don't know
what else to do, I am just going to scream
as loud as I motherfucking can. I am going to scare
all the birds from the trees, crush their wings
in my hands and turn my room into a graveyard
of talons and beaks, slit my wrists, saw my teeth
down to their roots, set a fetus on fire in the middle of my bed
and lie down next to it, so I can wake up sweating
in a sea of nightmares for the rest of my life, so my brother
won't have to do this alone.

Whoever Decided It Was a Good Idea for Lovers to Cohabitate

must've been out of their mind.
Because although it might seem like a good idea at the time,
and you can imagine how sweet it would be
to make love on the table you ate dinner at a few hours before,
the table you bought together, the dinner he helped you cook
with the food he helped you pick out, and how nice
to later curl up in the same bed, the curve of your ass snug
against the seat of his groin, his hand
draped across your waist as you both slip into dreams you don't care to
  remember in the morning
when you sneak up on him in the shower, work your fingertips
from his nipples to his hips and kneel
to catch the beads of water rolling off his skin onto your tongue—you know,
start his day off right so he'll think of you at work—
eventually, you get tired. At night, his arm
is heavy, his skin, hot,
too hot, like summer sometimes, sticky and
suffocating, no matter how cold the beer is. And you begin to notice
his pubic hairs on the toilet when you lift the seat to clean it,
and you feel your face tighten as you spray cleaning solution at the curly
  strands,
hoping the stream is strong enough to knock the hairs into the toilet
so you don't have to touch them,
and you feel like an exterminator, the way you aim and squeeze so hard,

or like a stranger in your own bathroom, a housekeeper,
the way you wish you had rubber gloves, the way
you cringe at the dried splashes of piss, and you remember
that the color yellow has always made you sad,
and you've never been able to explain that but suddenly
it makes sense, and then you stand up
and wonder aloud why you didn't think to get some damn gloves,
and although you've always loved bathrooms for their acoustics,
this time you hate the tiled walls for giving you nothing more than the echo of
your own stupid voice.

Someone Left out in the Rain

I'm so fucking tired I might as well be drunk or try to write
in my sleep, but I keep thinking about this thread
running through the middle of my body and up
through my skull, drawing
me into the sky like
a marionette, except I don't think anyone
is pulling on the other end. And when I think very hard, I realize I can't see
the end of the thread, which is dark blue and disappears
about 50 miles above me, like the point
of a beam of light in a cave, which must be the place
this lonely feeling comes from, because I don't like to think
it could come from inside me, that I
could be so empty. But maybe that's what happens
when you spend Friday night working
at the liquor store, helping people decide what kind of drinks
they should serve at their Halloween parties, selling cheap beer
to old men in sweatpants, the woman
who just lost her job
at the Legion up the street, her mouth like a half-smoked cigarette
someone left out in the rain, her eyes
like aluminum cans someone
keeps crushing and
crushing. On the drive home I play a game with myself,
where I have to decide which scenario

I'd most enjoy going home to. In the first
I am a teacher, with a stack of papers to grade
and a bottle of Cabernet already opened and breathing
on the end table in the living room
where it's always nighttime and the windows
have red drapes and there's piano music
coming from the neighbor upstairs, the notes drifting through my ceiling
like royal dust from an 18th century party dress, a time when wide hips
were something to crave. But my drive is short,
and so my fantasies never get
much further than that, and really the whole point of the game
is to decide whether or not I wish I had someone
to go home to, a lap to fold into, a hand to hold, a body
to remind me of my own. Tonight I am so tired
I decide I don't want
to be reminded of anything, that I'm okay
with my job at the liquor store, feeling
both younger and older than I am, always scrubbing
at the numbers I've glued to myself so that
I always feel raw, like split knuckles
bleeding in the wind. I climb into bed
and decide I'm okay
with being alone in it, which feels like deciding
I'm okay with being dead, at which point the thread snaps, done
with its job for the night, my spine
collapsing like a tower down inside me.

The Wake

Because life is hard I've been sleeping
with my jaw clenched too tight, my tongue
jammed against the back of my teeth, my teeth
like a dam, keeping everything from
bursting out of my mouth like the broken
spring of a child's jack-in-the-box, which has to be
the cruelest toy ever invented. Its yellow melody rises
like fireflies, like God's teeth, the small sacs of pollen that sprout
from the insides of day lilies, only to moments later scare
the living fuck out of you, wrecking your stroll along the cotton
candy boardwalk of the daydreams
you'd only just begun, shattering
the very little sense you'd made of this world. I wonder
what I knew about the world, what light
flew out of my mouth when I was two
and friends of my parents came to visit,
placed a present on the floor in front me,
told me to watch what happened
as they wound the handle. I remember
being punched in the stomach, turning black
from the inside out, the gasp of the needle as it split apart
the molecule of darkness hidden inside me, spread it like oil
in the ocean, and maybe this is why I've never
enjoyed jewelry boxes that play music when you lift the lid, the poor

mini dancer trapped inside the most
bizarre coffin. I can feel her tiny toes like screws
twisting themselves into the skin of my neck every time
I hear an ice cream truck come rolling down the street, half-expecting Jack
to pop out of the roof of the truck like the bully
he is, lurking in tunnels at playgrounds and inside the pipes of the organ
on the vintage carousel at the state fair, always
with a single blow pushing me back into the corner
of my disappointments, my failures, out into the middle of the aisle
of the funerals of all the people I love, all the people
I'll outlive, down onto my knees, back onto the floor
of the apartment in Germany, where the toddler I was
is still screaming, already mourning
everything I'll ever lose.

The Morning after I Left

Maybe I should feel more sad but
I keep thinking about this red balloon, drifting
across a grassy field into the hot
blue sky, and how the color red makes my tongue
swell at the back of my throat, like an overripe raspberry
whose cluster of cells we all once resembled
as we grew inside our mothers, those early weeks, before
identity claimed us. In a memory that might have only been a dream,
I'm picking raspberries with my grandmother
on her farm in Germany, circa 1990, the year
my brother was born and Kate Moss
was beautiful in black and white. *Kate*
Moss, Kate Moss, Kate Moss, Kate Moss—I'm convinced
if I say her name enough times my mouth
will turn to silver, not the hard metal but
the mercury you find on the ocean at midnight
when the moon spreads its naked wings,
the sand on a lover's back, the wet, matted hair.
And I wanted to say that this morning I woke up
and realized that for the first time in my adult life
I am single, alone, as if yesterday morning
was really any different, as if yesterday morning
I was still wrapping my legs around you,
as if when I thought about lovers

on the beach it was your hair in my hands, your hands
in my mouth, as if yesterday I hadn't already been red
and burning away from us, like the balloon
in my brain, who knows how long it's been gone.

Blood Lines

Sometimes I wish you would run away
the way my birth father did, that stranger
without whose orgasm I wouldn't exist. I want you to run away
so that I can run away
with our daughter to a beach town
in northern California because I'm still young enough
to believe my shadow won't follow me there, that it's impossible
to be lonely in a place where it's always sunny, even though
it was sunny all those days we were on vacation in the Caribbean
last January, and I was lonely
next to you on one of the most beautiful beaches in the world,
so I started reading the book of poems
I'd brought along in my bag, and you got mad,
and later at dinner we both cried
and it wasn't the first time I felt like a moon
without a planet, but this time the sea between us was quiet and I had
no desire to cross it, only
for you to keep drifting
away like a sailboat in the wind I've stopped building a roof against.
And so probably I shouldn't have fucked you
in the car in the airport parking lot after we landed
back home in Minnesota, but it felt good and you know
I'm selfish like that, like my father, too selfish
to be a parent, is what you said

the day I left, which made it really easy
to hate you. And for the first time in my life
I welcomed hate, invited it in
for an after-dinner cocktail, ran my finger up its thigh and begged it
to stay the night, so that my dream of running away would feel less like a dream
and more like the right thing to do, so I could say
our daughter doesn't need you
the way I know she does
because only you can teach her
to be less like me at night when I move my pillow
a little to the right so hate can lay
down beside me, so I can grip it by the hips
and let it whisper in my ear all night, let it strip
the tenderness from you like meat
from the bone, so for a moment I feel I understand
something about war, here in the dark between the sheets, where hate
moves its rough mouth hard against mine and I start
to taste blood and like it.

On Elbows

I’ve come to realize that much of my loneliness
is my own fault. At parties I should try harder
to talk to people but instead just imagine what it might
be like to kiss them. Isn’t it strange: I’ve never
kissed anyone with a beard, or even a goatee.
I’ve never kissed a woman or a gay man and not
that I necessarily want to but you can’t help
but wonder about these things, about the guy
with the thick bottom lip, or the one with the tongue
ring that flashes like a songbird in the sun when he laughs.
I’ve never kissed anyone not white, although my first
marriage proposal was from a black boy named Aaron.
We were in first grade and I liked him too but was so
socially awkward that all I could do was take the golden
quarter-machine ring which he’d so bravely offered
and throw it into the empty metal trash can
in front of the teacher’s desk. If my heart had a door-
bell it’d be that dull clang of metal on metal, the slow
thud of the self folding in on itself over and over again,
dragging itself on its elbows through the mud like
a soldier with no legs, a screaming mouth with no face,
the self folding and falling and crashing and crawling until all
that’s left is a misshapen accordion-like object
that no one knows what to call and would probably infect

you with tetanus if you stepped on it. It's the end of the party and I've kissed almost everyone who looks clean enough. It's the end of the party and I've spoken to almost no one. It's the end of the party and I'm going home like I always do: Alone, and exhausted.

Pinot Noir

And just like that I'm tired of summer, ready
for fall, which confuses me because it's only July
and wasn't I just dreaming
in hot blue letters, about golden
bodies fucking on the beach under
the sun? Didn't I just spend too much money
on a pair of sunglasses I didn't need but wanted because they made me feel
like I belonged in California? Wasn't I just soaking
wet between my breasts and didn't I just love it, the beads
of sweat like silver, like atoms from the mouths of hot planets
rolling down my body, which is tan, which I should
be happy about because in six months I will be white and there will be snow
and my brother
will be at war and so this year I'll be even sadder
than I always am when it's winter and the holiday parties
are over and all the young kids in college
will start planning their spring breaks
on the beach, the thought of which hums
like a pink and yellow neon sign in my brain because it's something
I've never experienced, and all the nice families
will go on their nice family vacations
to places like Disney World or maybe
the cabin up north or skiing
in Colorado, which I would love to do

if I could ski, if I wasn't
missing the family part, which I wasn't missing
a few months ago, when I was still able
to be housewife, mother, lover, dog-shit picker-upper, interior
decorator, and how grateful I was
for the IKEA furniture in our bedroom, how the houseplants
in the east-facing bay window were so green and beautiful it hurt
my chest to look at them, and the organic
Greek yogurt, the bamboo cooking spoons, the big
white bowls I would fill with fruit and honey
and flaxseed, and how I told myself
it was enough, I said *Look*
at what you have, you
are loved, you should
be happy, what
the hell is wrong with you? And of course I don't know
the answer to that, or to anything, really,
except that how I'm feeling right now is sexy like Giselle in the midnight
blue grip of these jeans and I keep thinking
about knee-high suede boots and how Riesling
is too sweet and all I really want is to drink Pinot Noir on the rooftop
of an old apartment in an old city, alone and watching the last light burn out
under the low clouds, the smoky
purple of autumn, the way it wraps itself around my heart
like bathwater, spilled ink, the glowing room I'll later curl up in while the indifferent
wind beats leaves against the ground, the windows and the walls, how it will hold me.

When People Ask If I'm Going to Give Evelyn a Brother or Sister

I say "No" and they look at me as if my mouth is full of staples. As if not wanting another child means I hate the one I have. It's true: I don't want more stretch marks because I hate the ones I have. There's a photograph that's been circulating on the Internet lately, of a woman proudly bearing her stretch marks saying something about being a tiger and having earned her stripes. Though I wouldn't feel less of a mother without mine. Sometimes I ask Google *Are single children more or less happy than children with siblings?* I think about my siblings, how my little brother is going to Afghanistan soon, and how I would put stretch marks on my face if it meant he'd be safe. I'd wear them like earrings. I'd eat them for breakfast if it meant that my 13-year-old sister never looked in the mirror and thought she wasn't good enough. It scares me how much control I have over my daughter's life. How much I don't.

Bear

Last night I woke up and in my half-sleep I
thanked God for this big comfortable bed,
and in the morning I thought that was weird
because I never
talk to God with intention like that,
but maybe it's because I've been trying
to open my chest
a little bit more, to untie all the
bad feelings like
balloons from my ribcage, let them sink
into the sky as I make
my bones soft and sink into myself, say every-
thing is okay. And it makes me nervous
to talk about things with capital letters, to think
about myself as being
okay, even though I'm always saying
I just want to be okay, even though my therapist
says I'm okay, and I take his words
home with me to sleep on, the big
overstuffed pillows that they are, his voice like
the belly of a bear I rub
my face against for an hour every week.
And every week we put all four
of our hands inside me, like archaeologists, I hand him

a piece of my rib and together we blow
off the dust and read it like braille, draw peace signs and hearts
in red and purple Sharpie
before we snap it back in place, and I'm so glad
I'm not attracted to him
enough to want to flirt, although he did say that thing
about the hippies getting it right, about freak flags and Einstein, about bending
time and how we're hanging
in space like a ball inside a net, wrapped in a thick
sticky cosmic hug, and I can't help but wonder
about the universe inside him, if he thinks I'm pretty and what
kind of animal
he's most closely related to, though I'd rather
not think of him as an animal at all but
a small bronze Buddha
I pray to every week, something
I can put on my dashboard or in
a bed of pink flowers, like the universe
itself, I'd rather
not think of him as someone who gets sad like me
because then I'll keep
falling all apart, like a letter
that's been folded for years, worn thin and stained blue
from the corners of your pocket. I'm always wondering
what's in other people's pockets, always tied
to everyone's feelings, like a puppet

with strings on every finger and every
toe, strings through my eyelids and strings through my cheeks, my mouth
like a maniac, a big red clown, I'm always
about to explode like a star, which is really
very beautiful, all that bright light
rushing into your eyes
from a million years away,
except that I'm a person
and it really fucking hurts
to have your limbs pulled out of their sockets,
and so I'm learning
how to keep myself together, how to be
even more selfish
than I already am, to think
about my therapist's feelings like horse-
flies, how if I have to I'll
swat them with a newspaper
or my shoe, feed them to a lizard or dip them
in honey and eat them myself, lick my fingers clean and growl.

Bruises

Today I am staying in my T-shirt and underwear
with so much sadness
in every ounce of my body, like being cradled
in the achy arms of the flu, and because there is nothing
else to do, I might as well climb onto the rooftop
and think about flamingoes, whose wild pink wings have been flashing
across the white sky of my brain all week for no apparent reason. I might even
light a cigarette. I might even smoke it. I might even call
the first friend I made in college, the poet
who bought me wine and kissed me on the cheek, said I looked
just like his ex-girlfriend and wouldn't I like
to be his supermodel? Why not be his supermodel
and traipse across the tightropes of his world in six-inch stilettos with a
martini in one hand
and a silk necktie in the other, wear lipstick and make movies
in the living room of his dreams? I wonder if wearing lipstick
would make me feel older. Right now I feel like a living room
that needs to be rearranged. My knees keep knocking
into my nerves, which keep tripping
over my anorexia and into
my arms. I hate that I have to keep reminding myself
that I am an adult. I hate that I don't know
what that means. If Victoria's Secret knew everything about sexy
they wouldn't be selling bras. Just white T-shirts

and mango-flavored chapstick. Movies of men cooking dinner while outside
an end-of-August storm creeps over the horizon like a bruise
on your spine you didn't know was there but like
to press up against because it makes you feel like you've done
something. This morning I got the mail from the mailbox
and that was something. I got a letter and that made me happy
but then I realized I had to open it
and I was sad, like tearing apart the seams
that keep a secret, when I opened the letter I thought I heard the sharp
first cry of a newborn, and so from now on I want to keep all my letters
unopened and next to my pillow forever, so that even after I die
they will always be there, the little pile of envelopes
with their little heavens breathing inside.
When I think about heaven I imagine
walking naked into the field across the street where
it's 1968 and I'm somewhere in Canada
taking pictures of all the small white flowers licking at my ankles so I can
  make postcards
to send to all the people who live far away, all the people
I'm always thinking of, which is everyone,
every day. When I think about heaven I feel
the way my daughter must feel when she sees
I've been crying and offers me her tiny body
to hold. When I think about heaven I think maybe
I should stop thinking altogether and move through the rest of the day
like the water that makes up more than half
of our bodies, how it moves

like a moan through the dark, curving
over the lip of a cup, holding on to itself longer than seems possible,
until the break, the spill, the tiny crash of the drip
of an IV next to the bed like the one that I'm in where
my veins are really no more
or less blue than yours, all these bruises
on my body from an ocean no one has named.

Sad Circus Tents

It's raining again and somewhere a two-year-old
is dying in the hospital because yesterday someone
beat the two-year-old and I
don't know why that happened. The government is shut down and I feel like
an idiot
because I don't even know what that means. Probably my brother
isn't getting paid. Probably someone is making bombs in the basement.
Probably the president wants to die. I can't keep track
of all the bad things happening right now
but it feels like spitting on the two-year-old's grave
if I just turn and look the other way like they keep
telling me I need to do. Put on the pretty pink glasses and look
at the pretty pink wall. Look at your pretty pink self.
The trees are weird colors, it's a motherfucking miracle.
I keep saying that. I keep breathing.
Are you going to live forever now?
My therapist says he's proud of all the progress I've made and I tell him
if someone dies I'm going
to move into his office and sleep on a cot beneath his desk,
turn myself inside out and wait for someone
to throw me in with the laundry. Put me in a laboratory.
Label all my parts and glue me to the inside of a pretty glass box.
Tell me what all these parts were made for and what
if the breathing doesn't work?

Breathing doesn't always work.
I think about telling the two-year-old's mother to breathe, and feel
like a bitch. I let her slap me. I let her sob into my arms and beat my chest
with her fists until my lungs collapse like the sad
circus tents that they are, standing bright red in the rain as if that could ever
make it stop.

Cat Lady

And it wouldn't be the strangest thing
if I never had sex again, but that's because I'm having
sex all the time, my eyes like two clits, my ears
like two clits, my mouth .... Today I'm drinking
coconut tea and looking at photos
of women I've never met, their spines like hybrids
between xylophones and violins, throats like galaxies, all the moons
sleeping in their bellies, and I wonder
why I'm not a lesbian, why
I don't want to reach out and touch them.
Then again I don't really
want to touch anyone. I sort of want you
to want to touch me, but not
enough to let you. I'm like that old
cat lady in an apartment on the dirty
outskirts of a city, except that I'm embarrassingly
young and all my cats
live inside me and they look
more like black-scaled fish and clouds
of plum smoke, small sequin purses and cherry
red mouths, my circus, my kingdom
of freaks. Last night we all
had a party in my bed. It was really sort of awful, the fish
unable to sit up straight and the mouths

without throats, no voices, just all of us sitting there together, hanging
open in the dark. Maybe it was more
of a funeral than a party, the way it hurt
to look at each other, how much
we needed to. I was holding a dead bird and pretending
it wasn't dead. I was wearing blue polka-
dot underwear, thinking
about my therapist, trying
to lighten the mood. I stuck
my finger in my belly button and said "Hey guys, every-
thing is okay, I promise," and then I fell
back onto the mattress, thought about Buddha and turned
myself into an enormous
ear, splayed my legs like butter-
fly wings, tried to listen for the vibrations of the invisible
strings holding us in space, holding
me together. But what
is holding me together and how
do I know that I am? Didn't I say
there was no such thing? I want to
stop saying so much but whenever I shut up all I hear is the hum
of air rushing through me. I hear a rustling like moth
wings, cotton sheets, like Love, the beautiful
woman in bed next to me, turning
her face to the wall the way I used to
with you, sobbing into her hands like a mother.

The Shape of a Heart

I want to text you naked photos from the bathroom,
lick an ice-cream cone while making eyes at you,
be stupid and cute. And by stupid I mean stop thinking
about cemetaries and morgues, stop wondering
how quickly bones freeze in the winter, and what happens
to the marrow inside, if it dries up like old fruit or
just evaporates into nothing, like all these words
coming out of my mouth, I've got nothing
to say because I can't stop thinking about the five kids
who just burned to death in Minneapolis
because of a space heater. Because God may
or may not exist. Because fire is hot and bodies melt
when they're on fire. Because we
are inside our bodies and without
our bodies we are nothing. Soon I will be nothing.
I don't have a television because it's where the news
comes from, which is almost always bad,
one more white cross on the side of the road and
my nerves will sputter out completely, my organs
come tumbling down the street like
balloons from a birthday party gone wrong.
It's winter and I love you and
you'll die someday too, a fact that will never
not make me cry. It's 2014 and

breathing is still painful, all that clean air
filling up my lungs, except the air's not really clean,
and most people aren't that smart,
and right now there are living rooms spilling over with blood,
and right now half the world is covered in light,
and right now there are machine guns
strapped to the chests of young boys,
and right now there are girls
being raped by those boys, those boys
raped by men who used to be those boys.
Fuck the circle of life. Wake me up when your heart
is the shape of a heart, when the bluebird
in your chest decides to be real,
takes a mouthful of dirt with its song.

May

I've been trying to do what I think are normal things,
like meet friends for dinner,
and laugh at people's jokes. I even texted
a boy about getting a drink sometime, but I can still feel
my nerves as if they were metal
wires sewing my top and bottom jaws
into a laboratory specimen. I still feel
like a prisoner without bars, as if someone
released me from somewhere too soon. I keep forgetting
how to spell. I'm slowly
tonguing my teeth and feel they might break
apart at any moment, all the tiny earthquakes
waiting in my bones. I keep looking out the window,
where this past week all the trees went hysterical, like preteens in puberty, it's so obnoxious
how green they are, how much I want
this green to be enough for me, this oxygen, this pretty
swollen May. But I'm terrified of these days
when flowers are just flowers, just more shit
taking up space. I keep crying. I keep thinking
about going for a walk
in the woods by a lake called Anne, but it's already 2:30 in the afternoon
and I'm too nervous to get dressed, too nervous
to eat, too nervous to actually have a drink or respond to

these men who keep calling me, sending nice messages
and pictures of flowers. They are so sweet and I
want nothing to do with them, at least not directly, at least not in a way
that holds me responsible for some-
one's feelings or something. I have enough
feelings of my own that I'm supposed to
start taking better care of, like children, I'm supposed to
hold them to my chest and feel their frantic hearts
beat against my steady
one, to swaddle them in domestic
cotton and sing them
to sleep, let them go the way I have
to learn to let my daughter go, the way she's been going
from me since before she was born, the way the clouds
always go, moving like a parade of elephants across the sky, the sky whose
  bright blue
has nothing to do with me.

Party of One

I closed the door behind you and all the windows
broke open, all the pianos
I've always wanted to play
stood in the street below, their soft mouths
opening and closing as they fumbled
for notes to fill the holes in the air tearing
apart around me, like flowers
with fingernails, scratching
themselves to dust. I was afraid
to move, that I might fall
through the floor and die or crash
into the shadow moving around the room, the absence
of you, that if I touched it
I'd drown in the ocean
roaring in my ears, the echo
of my name in your mouth, that I'd be carried
like a shell through time, washed up
on the beach of some planet spinning
at warp speed in a place in the universe so dark even black holes
are afraid of getting lost there. But of course
I moved. I blew my nose. I emptied
your coffee cup and felt like I was digging
a grave. And then the room was a grave
and all my loneliness shoveled itself on top of me, my first taste

of the dying body
that I am. And now that I've tasted it, I don't know
if I'll ever climb all the way out, if enough of your kisses
could clean this dirt from my teeth, if there's a piano in the world
that wouldn't break
under the weight of this song, this life, this party
of one. The sky is a bag full of midnight-
blue bricks, emptying down around me, and I don't remember
being invited. I don't remember
saying yes.

Acknowledgements

First and foremost I would like to thank everyone at University of Hell Press who worked hard to make this book happen:

Greg Gerding, Tyler Atwood, and Eve Connell for editing and proofreading with incredible insight and dedication to every last comma; Amy Chadwick for providing additional editorial support and back cover copy; and Vince Norris for the overall design and layout. An added special thank you to Greg Gerding for involving me in every step of the process and letting me know that U of Hell supports me in my creative work and beyond.

I would like to thank Susannah Kelly for her astounding illustrations on the cover and throughout the book, adding a visual layer to my poems I never imagined and am so moved by.

Thanks also to Vermont College of Fine Arts and my poetry mentors Jody Gladding, Leslie Ullman, Rigoberto González, and especially Matthew Dickman for showing me how to make so many of these poems breathe.

To my friends—most of you are on the Internet—now I am in your hands. Thank you.

"Hello Hello" and "Bruises" first appeared in *Split Lip Magazine.*

"RSVP," "All the Birthday Candles," and "Someone Left Out In the Rain" first appeared in *Country Music.*

"This Morning the Dew on the Grass Was So Beautiful" first appeared in *The Bakery.*

"Crush" and "Coil" first appeared in *B O D Y.*

"November" first appeared in *Poetry City USA, Vol. II.*

"While I'm Busy" first appeared in *Bare Hands Poetry.*

"Smoke" and "Everything Beautiful Happens in My Mouth" first appeared in *Narrative Magazine.*

"Down Into the Grass" first appeared in *Connotation Press.*

"Unborn" and "Big Spoon I Keep Wetting My Lips Against" first appeared in *Northwind Magazine.*

"Professionals" first appeared in *Phantom Limb Press.*

"Red Paper Heart" first appeared in *Metazen.*

"Moon Dog" first appeared in *smoking glue gun.*

"The Smaller I Become in It" first appeared in *The Medical Journal of Australia.*

"Daisies the Size of Moons," "Rain Poem," and "All the Birds From the Tress" first appeared in *H_NGM_N.*

"When People Ask If I'm Going to Give Evelyn a Brother Or Sister" first appeared in *PANK.*

"On Elbows" first appeared in *MiPOesias.*

"To a Real Party" and "The Wake" first appeared in *Paper Darts.*

"Sad Circus Tents" first appeared in *Ampersand Review.*

"This Is What It's Like To Fall Out Of Love" first appeared in *anderbo.*

About the Author

Sarah Xerta was born in Germany in 1987 and has since called many places home, none of them permanent. She is the author of the chapbooks JULIET (I) (H_NGM_N Books, 2014) and RED PAPER HEART (Zoo Cake Press, 2013). She received her MFA from Vermont College of Fine Arts and currently lives near Minneapolis, Minnesota. Find more of her work at sarahxerta.com.

This book is one of the many available from University of Hell Press. Do you have them all?

by Tyler Atwood
an electric sheep jumps to greener pasture

by John W Barrios
Here Comes the New Joy

by Eirean Bradley
the I in team
the little big book of go kill yourself

by Calvero
someday i'm going to marry Katy Perry
i want love so great it makes Nicholas Sparks cream in his pants

by Leah Noble Davidson
Poetic Scientifica

by Rory Douglas
The Most Fun You'll Have at a Cage Fight

by Brian S. Ellis
American Dust Revisited
Often Go Awry

by Greg Gerding
The Burning Album of Lame
Venue Voyeurisms: Bars of San Diego
Loser Makes Good: Selected Poems 1994
Piss Artist: Selected Poems 1995-1999
The Idiot Parade: Selected Poems 2000-2005

by Lauren Gilmore
Outdancing the Universe

by Rob Gray
Immaculate/The Rhododendron and Camellia Year Book (1966)

by Joseph Edwin Haeger
Learn to Swim

by Lindsey Kugler
HERE.

by Wryly T. McCutchen
My Ugly and Other Love Snarls

by Michael McLaughlin
Countless Cinemas

by Johnny No Bueno
We Were Warriors

by A.M. O'Malley
What to Expect When You're Expecting Something Else

by Stephen M. Park
High & Dry
The Grass is Greener

by Christine Rice
Swarm Theory

by Michael N. Thompson
A Murder of Crows
Days of Swine and Roses

UNIVERSITY OF HELL PRESS

CPSIA information can be obtained
at www.ICGtesting.com
Printed in the USA
FFHW020148120319
50915945-56337FF